About the author

MICHAEL MCTAGUE has been studying poetry for many years. This book represents a shift to creating poetry. He completed his doctoral dissertation at the University of Iowa by comparing translations of *Beowulf*. His studies span medieval and modern literature as well as Old Norse, Dante and Latin works. Over the years, he has taught many courses in literature, writing and business. He is the author of *The Businessman in Literature: Dante to Melville*, published by The Philosophical Library.

A New York native, his poems draw from a variety of experiences in and out of the largest city in the US. Dr. McTague has taught many college-level courses. He also studied Poetics with the Pulitzer Prize winning American poet, James Wright.

He spends a good deal of his time working at a private equity firm in New York. In this role, he has worked with companies in energy, pharmaceuticals, medical equipment, travel services, mining, higher education and other industries to secure financing. He has written numerous articles on business and contributes to Equities.com. You can find him on an Amazon author's page. In 2020, he published *Secrets of Effective Business Plans*.

POEMS FROM THE TOP OF THE WORLD

MICHAEL MCTAGUE

POEMS FROM THE TOP OF THE WORLD

Vanguard Press

VANGUARD PAPERBACK

© Copyright 2021
Michael McTague

The right of Michael McTague to be identified as author of
this work has been asserted by him in accordance with the
Copyright, Designs and Patents Act 1988.

All Rights Reserved

No reproduction, copy or transmission of this publication
may be made without written permission.
No paragraph of this publication may be reproduced,
copied or transmitted save with the written permission of the publisher, or
in accordance with the provisions
of the Copyright Act 1956 (as amended).

Any person who commits any unauthorised act in relation to
this publication may be liable to criminal
prosecution and civil claims for damages.

A CIP catalogue record for this title is
available from the British Library.

ISBN 978 1 80016 070 5

Vanguard Press is an imprint of
Pegasus Elliot MacKenzie Publishers Ltd.
www.pegasuspublishers.com

First Published in 2021

Vanguard Press
Sheraton House Castle Park
Cambridge England

Printed & Bound in Great Britain

Table of Contents

Foreword 9

The Gate of Hell 11

Botticelli's Venus 13

The Hawk of Point Pleasant 14

Return to Sender 16

Hekla 17

There's Money in Poverty 20

The Hallicrafter 23

Calling the Roll 26

The Gondola 29

The Icelandic Poppy 31

Modern Pilgrims 32

An Old Cumberland Street Beggar 34

Those Movie Lines 36

Yearbook 37

Another Cold Morning 39

Foreword

This collection of poems spans various matters. It touches on contemporary themes and stretches back to subjects from the Middle Ages.

As a student of James Wright and others, the author seeks to please and inform readers.

Michael McTague

The Gate of Hell

More ominous than Fuji's obscuring clouds
Or Kilimanjaro's snows is the cold darkness
That shrouds my angry presence.
More terrifying than Everest's wind and closeness
To the gate of heaven.
More remote than Pompei, pestered by rich
tourists.

All fools avoid my realm: bird watchers,
Rock climbers, searchers for gold and oil.
I am Hekla, the greatest mountain, Gate of Hell.
The border crossing that welcomes all travelers,
transporter of souls.

Burning fury created me. Inside those crevices
Now so quiet once raged spurting lava.
I protect my solitude. Fear, darkness and ice are
the artifices
I employ to ward off meddlers.
No bird visits. Watch their low approach and rapid
departure,
Shunned by icy shadows. No plants, no sheep
graze,
Bad roads, no human life for miles, only my
demeanor.

Beyond Gabriel Garcia Marquez's love of solitude.
Protected by an ash desert, protruding above a wide,
Dry emptiness. No clanging gate, merely an eerie quiet.
For centuries, I ply my trade out of sight.

I looked down upon the Viking ancestors of this tiny country.
Burning, killing, stealing. Returning from their savage plunder.
They rowed across the wine dark sea. I smiled.
We are family.
Watching. Seeing all. Reigning through fear.

Seizing the dead in the gloom of night.
I alone control the end of life, the departure from joy and order.
I remain the Master of Terror.

Botticelli's Venus

Propelled by the wind, floating effortlessly
To shore. Right foot aloft, eyes devoid of focus.
Unborn. Fully formed as was Eve.
No knowledge. No fear. No joy. No memory.
Tabula rasa completely empty.
Sans childhood. Born into a world of summer
An opulent swaddling cloth awaits on shore
In a Renaissance garden full of orange trees.

All will change when you alight on terra firma.
Goddesses are few and far between.
Where is your monarchy? Deo gratia, regina.
Born too early or too late? What will be your fate?
War, hunger, disease may intervene
Can you wait for democracy?
Who would be your equal in a world between new and old
Where beauty is so often squandered?

The Hawk of Point Pleasant

Across Point Pleasant, Brielle and Manasquan
The hawk reigns. No eagle or falcon violates my dominion.
My limits are my own. I shun seagulls
And leave them to snatch killies and fish heads.

Mark me! Do not compare me to lesser birds.
I am no falcon who gives up his freedom to men
The falconer fears me and I despise him.
No cage holds me. I use my wits and my claws to stay free.

Below, thirteen blackbirds watch men and women.
All the better for me who glides in silence unseen.
Selecting the company of the night. After the day's turbulence.
No man challenges my hegemony.

Everywhere below is neatness; all matters are set.
Grass skirts the sidewalks like a crew cut.
I fly above. No one escapes my ken.
I own twilight and observe all men,

Living beyond human passion

The doctor's Cadillac, The mother's pain.
Beneath my gaze a baby will be born.
The name of Dottie's offspring will be Sharon.

I take wing over the home of the one beneath the elms
He who knows mourning. Along the unpaved lane
That winds toward the wide porch.
Damp air, early shadows intrude on that human heart
Kin are we, offspring of ones who lament.
I live in a hunter's land, an outcast ruler here
I do not migrate. Tenderness has no part of me.
I see all. I terrorize, but I do not feel.

Return to Sender

I sent an email to a friend. In cyberspace it disappeared.
The Internet did not recognize a life departed.
"Invalid recipient" is the only recognition
She received from the social media vehicle
That links billions across the web
No likes for her. She is now at "invalid" status.
Reduced to an "error message".

So much the Internet does not know!
More than an email address, she was a real person
Thoreau her specialty. She understood
Why he built that lonesome cabin.
What private yearning drew him to the pond
And across Maine woods. She knew what stirred
That lonely heart to a life of solitude.
Watching the ice choppers from the isolation
Of a reconstructed shed

Solitude demands recognition.
Those who retreat do not abandon the world.
They only stand apart a little way to inspire
Us and make us know that life demands
Private thoughts, quiet time
A touch of seclusion where feelings develop.
The dispenser of knowledge knows so little.

Hekla

Mount Hekla looks down on Europe
Seeing all from its lofty top
Eye hidden in the snow
Shielded by the cold and mist
That covers all great mountains
Watching over the world for centuries

From the wasteland, the volcano arose
Above the basin that formed the oceans,
Bulging above the land.
Out of darkness it sprang; sublime it remains.

The sun hangs on the distant horizon
Cattycorner across the earth
Summer sun in Iceland encamped
By a crimson band that tamps down human emotions

Two massive entities – the sun at
One corner, Hekla opposite
Its glistening ice coat darkening
All that sits in fear between

The great mountain watches life unfold

The Vikings returning with plunder, women and gold
Hundreds of whales dragged on land
Ripped apart for lamp oil and food.
Tons of herring yanked from boats.
The lava stones alongside the river at Seljalandsfoss
Shaped like chevrons mark it forever.

The birth of democracy at Thingvellir
Among those grey, barren stones,
A small waterfall rolling down
To a peaceful stream
You heard the words of Snorri Sturluson
Watched Bergthora and Gunnar working the land
Einar, Helgi and Floki returning with spoils

At your feet you watched
As Skarphethin burned in his booth.
The moss, ponies and sheep
That wander and graze nearby
Cannot soothe you.
You remember the blood and fire.

Miles of lava insulate you better than a mine field,
More secure than an army or a missile defense.

There's Money in Poverty

What business starter or itinerant scholar
Sits idly waiting for the dole
Breathing heavily as they call the roll
Merely a number in a slow computer

Listen up everyone. Turn off smart phones.
Remove ear buds. No boom boxes
The rules of the game are posted.
To get your stipend, you must show photo ID
Date of birth, current employment status,
Driver's license. Have all available for analysis.

Veterans go to floor ten with DD214s
No ma'am. No cash payments. All disbursements
By direct deposit. We have no metro cards.
If you wish to file a complaint,
Ask for a packet or access the procedure on the Internet.
No, sir. Food stamps are handled on floor six.
No cash payments unless you document a crisis.

Just out of jail? Those who were incarcerated
Go to the Truman Room to be processed.
Take the elevator to the second floor.
Ask for the PO. Complete the questionnaire.

Ms. Washington is in conference.
Ask her assistant for an appointment.
Mr. Lincoln is on a site visit to Brooklyn.
If it's key, text the driver of his SUV.
Mr. Johnson has been waiting a long while
To access his newly renovated domicile.
Ms. Hoover needs funding for transportation.
Her metro card ran out. She demands verification.

All those applying for funding,
Follow me. Step onto the elevator.
For transport to the Roosevelt Room, fourth floor.
Those present for education and training,
Follow me to the Jefferson Room on floor seven.

Ms. Adams wants to enter the seamstress
Training program. The school bursar needs
Authorization to download the funds.
Ms. Wilson will be here at 2:00 precisely
She handles all monetary emergencies.

Sorry, the director is incommunicado. He's
lunching with the mayor.
Appropriations are the subject of their get together
To see him, call Mr. Clinton, his staff worker.

Mr. Arthur, your stipend will go overnight, UPS.
Ms. Grant, SNAP benefit funds are available
through Chase.
Mr. Pierce, keep your public assistance
Information private. You know, totally hush-hush.
Please be seated. We are all in a rush, Mr. Bush.

All those with stamped approval
Proceed to the controller's portal

Is this the end of our troubles,
People seeking government alms?

The Hallicrafter

Up in the rafters, there's a Hallicrafter
Its aerial roams out the window
Up to the roof, around the chimney
A mere piece of the past, full of dust.
Next to a red wagon caked with rust.
Fit for a glance on a tour, a blast from the past.

Long ago times are a funny thing.
Imagine those boobs, trying to delight in
Rock and roll from vacuum tubes.
At best, it squealed from jazz and swing
Powered by coils and springs.
Short wave they called it.
Across the entire dial that eerie pinging
Dots and dashes, relentlessly wailing
Above the ocean and beyond.
Do they carry any meaning?

Oh well. It's barely fit for a yard sale.
Belongs in the basement of a museum.
It lost the power to inspire
To set a soul on fire
The desire to inform, the nerve to move.
The tenacity to bring out ferocity.

We cannot bring the dead to life from old things
Students amble through gloomy rooms
Glancing at displays for school projects.
Mummies smile; but remain mute witnesses.
Vikings breathe, striving to please
Those who paid the entrance fees
Visitors depart saying invariably
They enjoyed an afternoon when they were free
Alas, age has limits.

Everywhere is the same.
In Rome, pilgrims kiss the feet of St. Peter.
Tourists crane their necks to admire the creation of Adam.
Flood lights illuminate the Coliseum.
At Lourdes, they rinse in the sacred water.

Who were the people who lived in times past?
Did they stare at the Pieta? Hug the column of Trajon?
Look in the face of a Fra Angelico composition?
Visit the Capitoline and the Forum below?
So many centuries in between.
We have the art but the people are gone.

How intently did our grandparents lean toward the Hallicrafter,

Hoping to hear H.V. Kaltenborn reporting.
Did he say the war was over?
The fight on the beaches is ending?
Edward R. Murrow reporting?
Soldiers climbing the cliffs of Normandy?
A fireside chat propelled across the ocean?
Who is sending those damned signals?

New conflicts engulf this world
Seeking information, we tune in.
Like our ancestors, bowing to the device.
Minds stirring, bodies anesthetized.
The past forgotten. Surpassed by the chip,
The smart phone and the Internet.

Calling the Roll

Everywhere the register is called.
School, army, census, end of life.
No time for day dreaming.
How many are missing?
Are those present
More precious than the absent?

<u>Cano</u>? How many centuries between you and the journey
From the coast of Troy to Italy?
How long *Italiae quī prīmus ab ōrīs* New York?
<u>Goldenberg</u>? Proud parents encourage more intellectual deeds.
Your sister is a scholar. Keep up the endeavor.
On graduation day, you must transcend.
<u>Khadija</u>? Eyes lowered, averted glance.
Ready to be a prophet's bride?
Not yet. Years of menial jobs intrude
<u>Li</u>? Odor of rice when you speak,
If you speak. Your parents are jubilant
You grow corpulent in this new habitat.
<u>McDermott</u>? Great grandson of the Easter Rebellion
Generations sever you from the conflict and the famine

How many Atlantic crossings and shattered dreams of fortune?
Daniel Ortega? You're no dictator.
Are you present or in a stupor?
Sleepy eyes tell of a long night of texting.
Polite? Absent for ten days.
Abandoning the members of the class team.
Your fellow students seek your input and wisdom.
Rivera? So many share your name.
How will you stand out from the throng?
Will learning bring you renown?
Schell? How did you come by the wrong name?
Silent, unlike the mortar that rains down
Seldom reacting. Angry and sullen.
Washington? Lanky shoulders, wide fingers, small waist.
Ready for a conflict? On a battle field?
Heading for a goal line? Or leaving Trenton behind?

Will anyone marked present remember this meeting?
As we lay dying, will even one of these think,
I was present. Aha! It meant something.

The Gondola

Three rode in a gondola. Only one remains.
Plagued by fears, the survivor tosses and turns.
What wisdom does one gain by tarrying in this life?
Sharpness of memory exceeds present scrutiny
The bright Venetian sun and lap of water;
The scratch of the oar endures.
I reach back forty years more clearly than yesterday

Like a crossword puzzle missing clues,
The recollection fails. Two travelers vanished.
The answer eludes,
Shrouded in the grey light of times past
Halting fruitless efforts
To seize the beauty of long ago images
The pain and joy of those events overlain
By a sweetness of yearning and distance.
Searching for a meaning keeps us whole.

The Icelandic Poppy

Can a flower speak? Ask the Icelandic poppy.
It makes its case as well as a Wall Street lawyer.
Unlike its cousins, it thrives in a land of winter
Enduring short hours of light from Freyr

Long stems rise above the frost
Varying in height, allowing each shoot
To soak up nourishment from rain or snow.
The bowl shaped flowers drink the flow
Welcoming the warmer spring or autumn.
The melting snow drips down to the shorter members.
Talk about conservation! But it can't be renewed.
The thrifty poppy drinks up all moisture.
Roots gulp steadily below the dirt
Above the snow, it uses its little grey cells
To create beauty in total darkness.

Starved in winter gloom, summer light is magnified
In the end, its beauty enveloped by darkness. Shut down by Hodr.
For the Icelandic poppy, the labor is long but the splendor is short.

Modern Pilgrims

Tourists stand shoulder to shoulder before the Pieta
A reverent silence halts small talk. Older adults quiet their devices
The look of resolution on Mary's face and her lowered gaze reveal
Her recognition of the reality of the event: Christ has died.
Her left arm supports His torso. Her right hand open,
Beckoning scores of onlookers.
Her private pain collides with this most public event.

Visitors in the tour group immediately film the scene.
A few stare blankly. Two check the time.
One makes a joke. Another blesses herself.
The English guide from Tyrone speaks
Rapidly of Michelangelo's early life.

Two Americans stand in front, third year abroad students
From Terra Haute clothed in university sweatshirts to prove it.

The taller shakes his head from side to side.
"That dude could really cut stone," he opines.
His roommate nods. The pilgrims move on.
The stone figures do not even follow the pair
With their eyes as they amble toward St. Peter's
Chair.

An Old Cumberland Street Beggar

I came upon an old man snoozing on the sidewalk
On Cumberland Street in downtown Brooklyn.
Warmed by a tattered army jacket
His toes showed through holes in his Air Jordans.
His beard graying, arms sloping abruptly from the shoulder
Hinting at evaporated muscles.

A solitary warrior. No honor earned. No honor shown.
Partially obscured by a cold shadow
The kind that deters onlookers.
Eager for alms to visit McDonald's.
Discarded, shunned, a paltry thing.
Those he guarded do not love him.

A wide glance of the street shows no duffle bag
No sound of band or trumpet
No deuce and a half for transport.
Not even World War II K rations
Fitted out with tiny cigarette packs.

Local gentry pass by too busy to notice
The unmistakable horse, stripe and yellow field

Or to fill the hard palm of this piece of human war surplus.
That once carried an M-16 and occasionally an M-60.

Those Movie Lines

Raised voices mar the morning chitchat.
Managers irritated by another production stay
No bonuses. Not even an attaboy.
Is this the ultimate *failure to communicate?*

An overnight letter from the IRS
Someone filed a complaint? Fear rises.
The ones in charge ask your whereabouts
But, they *ain't got no stinking badges.*

Our competitor beat our sales again
We will roll out a special promotion
And give away a double coupon
Now you got the edge on him.

Wild eyes, mussed hair, wrinkled clothes
Office door closed all afternoon
Never heard the boss curse like that before.
You mean it really is the Russians?

Fired! After so many sleepless nights
Up 'til four a.m. at Wall Street summits
My brother generates all the hullabaloo
It was you, Charlie. It was always you.

Yearbook

The spine cringes after years on the shelf.
Aha. Black and white photos. So long ago.
Such dated technology.
Those serious looks. A few smiles.
Unsure of what lay ahead.

What killed that talented handful? Vietnam?
Disease? Accident?
Kenny, hit with flack five times. Or, was it eight?
Juan had cancer. They called it the big C back then.
Soft spoken Eddie. Became a police captain
Shot. In the line of duty, I suppose

Peter is doing well. Living in Boca Raton
Grandson in college. Waiting for the gravy train.
Big Kevin. Saw him a year ago.
Not so tall any more. Balding too.
Harry. Out of touch. Moved to Kansas City.
What a shock for his Delancey Street family.
Freddie. Dreamt of pro ball. Years of coaching in high school.
Willie, a funeral parlor owner's son.
No job search for him. Had it made from day one.

Look at me. Was I really that thin?
Lying awake at night, I take all under consideration
Do I deserve a page in this book of life?

Another Cold Morning

My nose is red; my phone is dead.
I shiver but cannot tell the temperature.
Those who travel with me are unaware
Cut off from what matters, unable to text until my battery renews

My bus will soon arrive; my nose runs.
I cannot see clearly. The destination reads, N—
I—S.
Hmmmmm! Ohhhhh! Not—In—Service.
I pine for phone and bus in vain. In limbo. How long must I remain?

The world passes by and I cannot converse
Disconnected from human company; it makes me furious
I said that yesterday and need a thesaurus.
The web is unavailable. I have no lexis

How paltry I feel, swaddled and muffled under grey skies
That withhold the sun and the critical URLs
I look east but travel west
Without Google Maps. I cannot run any apps.